Kaj Himmelstrup

Uncle Bill's Will

herausgegeben
von Klaus Stenzel

Ernst Klett Sprachen
Stuttgart

Kaj Himmelstrup

Uncle Bill's Will

herausgegeben von Klaus Stenzel

Performance permission
Permission to perform this play by students in school is hereby given.

1. Auflage 1 9 8 7 6 | 2019 18 17 16

Internetadresse: www.klett-sprachen.de

Gestaltung und Satz: Satzkasten, Stuttgart
Umschlaggestaltung: Elmar Feuerbach
Titelbild: iStockphoto
Druck und Bindung: CEWE Stiftung & Co. KGaA, Germering
Printed in Germany

ISBN 978-3-12-571361-1

Contents

Vorwort 7

Characters 8

Act 1 On board the pirate ship
'The White Skeleton' 9

Act 2 On the Golden Island 26

Vorwort

Uncle Bill's Will könnt Ihr wie eine ganz normale Geschichte lesen. Aber das wäre schade. Denn eigentlich ist es ein Theaterstück, das Ihr richtig aufführen solltet – vor der Klasse, vor der ganzen Schule oder vor den Eltern. Das macht etwas Mühe und viel Spaß, und Ihr übt Euer Englisch dabei!

Eine andere Möglichkeit ist, ein Hörspiel daraus zu machen. Das hat den Vorteil, dass Ihr Eure Rollen nicht auswendig zu lernen braucht – vor dem Mikrofon kann man seinen Text einfach ablesen. – Aber Ihr braucht einen „narrator" [nəˈreɪtə] – Erzähler, der alles das erklärt, was man sonst auf der Bühne sehen würde.

Schließlich könnte man ein Video aus *Uncle Bill's Will* machen, aber das ist gar nicht so einfach …

1 **will** letzter Wille, Testament

Characters

(Die Namen der auftretenden Personen sind keine echten, sondern sollen lustig wie Spitznamen sein.

Kate	Old Bill's niece
Jack	Kate's brother
Paul Pry	A customs officer

The Pirates

Captain Cannonball
One-eye
Claw
Skull
Bigmouth
Crossbone

Sailor 1
Sailor 2
Sailor 3
Sailor 4
Other pirates

The inhabitants of the Golden Island:

Pineapple
Coconut
Peach
Banana
Peanut

Orange
Lemon
Eight inhabitants
Other inhabitants

5 **customs officer** Zollbeamter – 7 **Cannonball** Kanonenkugel – 9 **Claw** Klaue (siehe Bild S. 30) – 10 **Skull** [skʌl] Totenschädel – 12 **Crossbone** über Kreuz gelegte(r) Knochen (siehe Piratenflagge S. 9) – 13 **inhabitant** Einwohner – 15 **Coconut** Kokosnuss – 15 **Lemon** Zitrone – 16 **Peach** Pfirsich – 18 **Peanut** Erdnuss

Act 1

The deck of the pirate ship 'The White Skeleton'. At the back of the stage is the side of the ship – about 70 cm high. On the left there is a cabin. On the deck a big chest, a sail, some rope. Kate's head appears above the side of the ship. She looks over the rail.

KATE: There's nobody on deck.

JACK: *(whispering)* Are you sure?

KATE: Yes, Come on.

JACK: *(appearing above the side, still whispering)* Is this the right ship?

KATE: Of course it is. Didn't you see the name? The White Skeleton.

JACK: Yes, but where's the pirates' flag . . . the skull and crossbones?

KATE: Don't be silly. When they're in harbour, they don't use the skull and crossbones.

The skull and crossbones

2 **stage** [steɪdʒ] Bühne – 3 **cabin** (Schiffs-)Kabine – 4 **chest** Truhe – 4 **sail** Segel – 4 **rope** Tau, dickes Seil – 4 **to appear** [ə'pɪə] erscheinen, auftreten – 5 **rail** [reɪl] Reling – 14 **flag** Flagge – 17 **harbour** ['hɑːbə] Hafen

JACK: Well, what are you going to do now?

KATE: Me? We! We are going to get on board. We must find the will. Come on. *(She wants to climb over the rail. Jack stops her.)*

JACK: No. Not now.

KATE: Why not? Are you afraid?

JACK: No. I'm not.

KATE: Yes, you are.

JACK: No, I'm not. I'm not afraid. Not at all.

KATE: Why don't we get on board then? We came here to find Uncle Bill's will and now you want to give up.

JACK: I don't think there is a will.

KATE: Oh no, typical!

JACK: Well, *I* have never seen it.

KATE: But Mum told us about it.

JACK: Well, *I* don't think it's true. And you? Do you *really* think he left all that money to the two of us?

KATE: That's what Mum said, and she knew all about it.

JACK: But what if Uncle Bill didn't have any money? What if it was all just a joke?

KATE: It isn't. I'm sure it isn't. I know he was poor when he died, but I'm sure the story of hidden treasure is true. You know, all his life he sailed around the world.

18 **true** wahr – 19 **to leave (left, left)** *hier:* hinterlassen, vererben – 26 **to die** sterben

JACK: But why did he leave it all on a desert island?

KATE: Don't ask me. I don't know. We only know that he made his will before he died. And the will says where the treasure is hidden.

JACK: Well, I don't believe it. There *is* no treasure.

KATE: Then why did the pirates steal the will? Mum is sure it was them. They want the treasure as much as we do. *(The cabin door opens. Kate and Jack hide behind the side of the ship. Crossbone comes through the door with a heavy bucket full of rubbish. He goes to the side of the boat and wants to throw the rubbish over the side. One-Eye comes through the cabin door, too, and Crossbone nearly hits him when he swings the bucket.)*

ONE-EYE: Watch out, you idiot.

CROSSBONE: Oh, I'm sorry.

ONE-EYE: What's in the bucket?

CROSSBONE: Rubbish. I'm cleaning the captain's cabin. Didn't you hear what he said this morning? We're going to leave today.

ONE-EYE: Yes, I did. He was talking about treasure and a desert island. Perhaps we'll be rich soon.

1 **desert** ['dezət] **island** einsame Insel – 15 **rubbish** ['rʌbɪʃ] Abfall – 20 **to swing** schwingen – 21 **watch out** pass auf!

CROSSBONE: That'll be the day! But it's going to be a long trip and we haven't got enough food on board yet. I'm going ashore to do some shopping.

ONE-EYE: You can't go ashore. You must stay here and keep watch.

CROSSBONE: Me? Why?

ONE-EYE: Because I'm going ashore. You're the only one on board then.

CROSSBONE: No, no, no. I'll buy the food. And you'll stay.

Cannonball ordered ME to go ashore.

ONE-EYE: Listen, friend, Captain Cannonball ordered me to go ashore and buy the drinks.

CROSSBONE: Well, I think food is more important than drinks.

ONE-EYE: Don't be silly. A pirate without rum is like a fish without water.

CROSSBONE: OK. I know what we'll do. We'll both go. Come on.

(Crossbone puts the bucket down.)

2 **trip** Reise – 5 **go ashore** [əˈʃɔː] an Land gehen – 6 **to keep watch** Wache halten – 13 **to order** befehlen – 17 **rum** [rʌm] Rum

CROSSBONE: After you.

ONE-EYE: No, after you.

(They leave the stage to the right. Kate and Jack come up again.)

KATE: Look, there's nobody here now. Come on.

(They climb over the rail)

Well, here we are.

JACK: Well, what now?

KATE: The Captain's cabin. We'll start there.

JACK: Kate! Listen! Someone is coming. Shhhh … Oh no, what are we going to do?

KATE: Hurry up. You get into the chest, and I'll hide under here.

(Jack gets into the chest and Kate hides under the sail. Captain Cannonball comes from the right with Skull, Bigmouth, and Claw.)

SKULL: Captain, Captain, where are we going?

BIGMOUTH: It's a secret, you idiot!

SKULL: But I'm so excited. I can't wait.

CLAW: Take it easy. Cannonball knows. That's enough for me.

SKULL: This story about treasure on a desert island, Captain, is it true?

BIGMOUTH: It's a secret, you fool.

CANNONBALL: Quiet. Sit down and I'll tell you.

(They sit down. Cannonball takes out his pipe.)

Where's the tobacco? I know we smuggled it on board last week.

31 **pipe** [paɪp] Pfeife – 32 **tobacco** ['təbækəʊ] Tabak – 33 **to smuggle** ['smʌgl] schmuggeln

SKULL: It's in the chest, Captain. Shall I get it? *(He gets up and goes to the chest. Just as he is going to open it Bigmouth takes out his tobacco.)*

BIGMOUTH: Have some of my tobacco, Captain.

CANNONBALL: It's all right. I'll wait. *(He puts his pipe back into his pocket and sits down on the chest.)* Now, you all knew Old Bill. Do you remember him?

SKULL: Old Bill … Ah, yes … We saved him when the good ship Marigold went down.

CANNONBALL: That's right. Now, where was the Marigold going when she went down? … She was on her way home from a far-away island … Do you remember that storm?

CLAW: What a storm!

SKULL: A hurricane!

BIGMOUTH: I'll remember it all my life!

CANNONBALL: Well, the Marigold went down and all the crew died ... all but one.

THE PIRATES: Old Bill!

CANNONBALL: Right … Old Bill! Do you remember how we found him?

SKULL: He was swimming in the open sea … we pulled him up and brought him home.

CANNONBALL: And what did he say?

CLAW: Thank you.

CANNONBALL: But he didn't say anything about treasure, right?

11 **to save** retten – 12 **Marigold … she** (Schiffe sind im Englischen oft weiblich.) – 20 **hurricane** [ˈhʌrɪkən] Orkan – 21 **life** [laɪf] Leben – 23 **crew** [kruː] (Schiffs-) Mannschaft – 23 **all but one** alle außer einem

THE PIRATES: Treasure?

CANNONBALL: Yes ... treasure ... He had hidden it on the island.

CLAW: And he never said anything to us!

CANNONBALL: I always thought Old Bill had a secret. And he didn't want to tell us.

BIGMOUTH: And where is he now?

CANNONBALL: He died a few weeks ago … before he could go back to the island. But he left a will and last night we stole it.
(He takes out an envelope. Paul Pry comes in and stands at the back of the stage.)

SKULL: Look, Captain. Here's somebody to see you.

BIGMOUTH: *(whispers)*
He's wearing a cap. He looks like a policeman.

SKULL: A policeman! Oh no!
(Cannonball puts the envelope in his pocket.)

BIGMOUTH: He's going to search the ship.
(He throws the rubbish under the sail, but he doesn't notice Kate.)

PRY: Good afternoon, Captain.

CANNONBALL: And who, sir, are you?

PRY: Pry, sir, Paul Pry, customs officer. I've come to have a look at your ship. May I come on board?

CANNONBALL: Of course.
(Pry climbs over the rail and steps on the sail.)

2 **had hidden** hatte … versteckt – 11 **envelope** ['envələʊp] Umschlag – 17 **cap** Mütze – 21 **pocket** Tasche – 22 **to search** [sɜːtʃ] durchsuchen – 31 **to step** treten

Kate: Ouch!

Bigmouth: What did you say?

Pry: I didn't say anything. Perhaps it was a rat.

(He wants to look under the sail.)

Cannonball: There are no rats on my ship.

Skull: Only a few mice.

Cannonball: What did you say?

Skull: Me? Oh … um … new rice … we've just got some new rice, sir.

Pry: Have you got anything to declare?

Cannonball: No, nothing.

Pry: No tobacco?

Cannonball: No, sir.

Pry: Perfume?

Cannonball: Perfume?

Pry: Yes, perfume.

(Pry sniffs around.)

Cannonball: We never use perfume.

(Pry sniffs his way to the chest.)

We NEVER use perfume!

7 **mouse,** *pl.* **mice** [maɪs] Maus – 9 **rice** [raɪs] Reis – 11 **to declare** [dɪˈkleə] verzollen – 15 **perfume** [ˈpɜːfjuːm] Parfum – 18 **to sniff** schnuppern

PRY: I think I can smell tobacco.
(Just at the moment when Pry is going to open the chest, Bigmouth takes out his tin of tobacco.)

BIGMOUTH: Look, sir, this is my tobacco ... it smells lovely, would you like some?

PRY: And have you paid duty on it?

BIGMOUTH: Of course we have. We bought it at the shop over there.

PRY: So you're not smugglers then?

BIGMOUTH: Us? Smugglers? How could you think that!

PRY: What about alcohol? Where are all the bottles?

CLAW: Bottles, sir?

PRY: Wine ... whisky ... rum ... beer?

SKULL: Oh no, sir. On this ship we only drink milk.

PRY: Oh really? ... Well, OK then.
(One-Eye and Crossbone come in from the right. One-Eye is carrying a heavy sack; Crossbone has got a big bottle. Pry goes to the sack. He hasn't seen the bottle.)
I'm a customs officer. What's in that sack?

1 **to smell** riechen – 7 **duty** ['djuːtɪ] Zoll – 10 **smuggler** ['smʌglə] Schmuggler – 13 **alcohol** ['ælkəhɒl] Alkohol – 16 **wine** [waɪn] Wein – 16 **whisky** ['wɪskɪ] Whisky – 16 **beer** [bɪə] Bier – 22 **sack** Sack

One-Eye: *(opens the sack)* Potatoes, cabbages, lemons, bread, and butter. Food for the trip, sir. *(Meanwhile Crossbone has given Skull the big bottle and Skull has hidden it in the chest. Skull hasn't seen Jack in the chest, and Pry hasn't noticed all this.)*

Pry: *(to Crossbone)* And what have you got?

Crossbone: Nothing, sir, nothing to declare.

Pry: Well, goodbye, Captain, and have a good trip.

Cannonball: Thank you, sir. Goodbye. *(Pry climbs over the rail and Leaves the stage. The rest of the crew arrive. They climb up over the side of the ship.)*

Sailor 1: Are we late, Captain?

Cannonball: No, you aren't.

Sailor 2: When do we leave, Captain?

Cannonball: In an hour or so, men.

Sailor 3: Is it going to be a long voyage, Captain?

Cannonball: A long voyage and a hard voyage.

Sailor 4: When will we come back, Captain?

Cannonball: Not this year, perhaps next year, but we'll all be rich men then.

Skull: The will, Captain. Read the will to us.

2 **cabbage** ['kæbɪdʒ] Kohl(kopf) – 4 **meanwhile** [ˌmiːn'waɪl] in der Zwischenzeit – 19 **sailor** ['seɪlə] Seemann – 23 **voyage** [vɔɪdʒ] (Schiffs-)Reise

CANNONBALL: *(Takes out an envelope, opens it, and takes out a piece of paper, too.)* Now listen. This is the last will and testament of Old Bill. *(starts to read)* "My name is Bill. All my life I've been a sailor. My last voyage was to the Golden Island with my friends of the good ship Marigold. We found treasure there, and we buried it. We were going back to the Golden Island because we wanted to bring our treasure back home. But there was a terrible hurricane. Our ship sank and all my friends drowned. A pirate ship saved only me and brought me back home. But now I am very ill. I will never sail again. My sister Mary is looking after me. When I die, I will leave all the treasure to my sister and her two children, Kate and Jack. With this letter, you will find a map of the Golden Island and it tells you where the treasure is." *(He puts the piece of paper back into his pocket.)*

SKULL: Don't stop, Captain, go on.

CANNONBALL: No. The rest is a secret.

CLAW: Cannonball knows. That's enough for me.

10 **to bury** ['berɪ] *hier:* vergraben – 14 **to sink (sank, sunk)** (ver-)sinken – 15 **to drown** ertrinken

CANNONBALL: Is everyone on board?
EVERYONE: Aye, aye, Sir.
CANNONBALL: OK. Cast off … Set sail … Skull, take the wheel … Claw, keep watch … We're leaving for the Golden Island.
(Everyone pulls on ropes in groups.)
BIGMOUTH: The sails are set, Captain.
CAPTAIN: Good. Come and sit down and we'll sing a song.

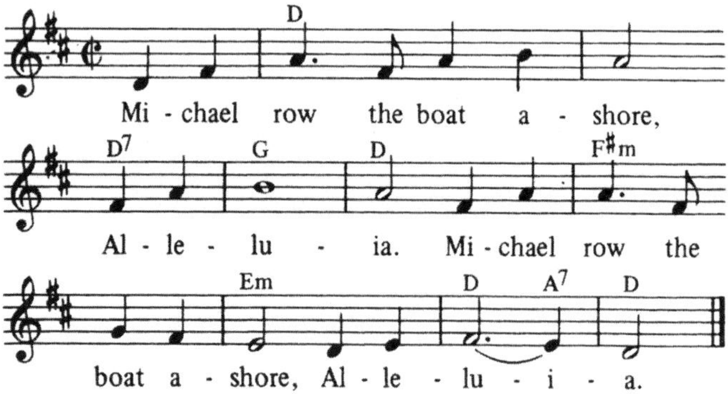

D = D
D^7 = D^7
G = G
F♯m = fis
A^7 = A^7
Em = e

3 **Cast** [kaːst] **off!** Löst die Leinen!

All: Michael, row the boat ashore
Al-le-lu-ia
Michael, row the boat ashore Alleluia
1. Sister help to trim the sail
Alleluia
Sister help to trim the sail
Alleluia
2. Jordan's river is deep and wide
Alleluia
Meet my mother on the other side
Alleluia
3. Jordan's river is chilly and cold
Alleluia
Chills the body but not the soul
Alleluia
4. Brother lend a helping hand
Alleluia
Brother lend a helping hand
Alleluia
5. Michael, row the boat ashore …

Cannonball: Come on, another one.

Skull: What'll it be?

Claw: Cannonball knows. That's enough for me.

Cannonball: What shall we do with the drunken sailor? … , wait a minute … we can't sing "what shall we do with the drunken sailor" without a drink … and it won't be milk!
(to Crossbone)
Did you get the bottle?

Crossbone: Yes, Captain. It's in the chest.

1 **to row** [rəʊ] rudern – 2 **allelula** [ˌælɪˈluːjə] (H)alleluja – 4 **to trim the sail** das Segel in den Wind stellen – 12 **chilly** frisch – 14 **body** Körper – 14 **soul** Seele – 16 **to lend a hand** helfen – 25 **drunken** betrunken

CANNONBALL: Open it up. Hurry up.

CROSSBONE: *(opens the chest)* Captain! There's somebody hiding here! A stowaway! Who on earth are you?

JACK: I'm Jack. *(He gives the bottle to Cannonball)* Is this your bottle, sir?

CANNONBALL: Thank you. How did you get into that chest? And why are you on my ship?

JACK: Er … there was a big dog, sir. It ran after me. I was afraid and hid in the chest.

CANNONBALL: Well, I've got some good news for you, young man. You're on your way to the South Sea, and you won't be home for a very long time … a very, very long time. Come on, boys, set more sail. *(Crossbone and One-Eye take the sail from the deck. They find Kate under it.)*

BIGMOUTH: Captain, we've found another one. Oh, she stinks. And who are you?

4 **stowaway** ['stəʊəweɪ] blinder Passagier – 4 **… on earth …** … um Himmels willen …

KATE: I'm Kate.

BIGMOUTH: Do you two know each other?

KATE: He's my brother.

JACK: And she's my sister.

BIGMOUTH: Don't be cheeky.

CROSSBONE: Well, Kate and Jack, what's your uncle called? I bet his name's Bill. Well? Answer me!

JACK: Yes, it is, you are right.

ONE-EYE: *(picks up two pieces of rope)* They must die, Captain. Let's hang them from the mast.

BIGMOUTH: Throw them into the water!

CLAW: Feed them to the fish!

CANNONBALL: No. I've got a much better idea. *(to Kate and Jack)* You wanted to go to the Golden Island and find the treasure, right?

JACK: Yes, we did.

KATE: And we still want to go there, Captain.

CANNONBALL: Then that's OK with me. Come with us to the island and help us to find the treasure.

CROSSBONE: Captain, that's impossible.

CANNONBALL: Well, why not? When we've found the treasure we'll come back home with it, *(to Kate and Jack)* and you two can stay on the island!

ONE-EYE: The desert island!

CANNONBALL: Come on, boys. It's time for a drink and another song. *(Crossbone ties Jack and Kate to the rail.)*

5 **cheeky** ['tʃi:kɪ] frech

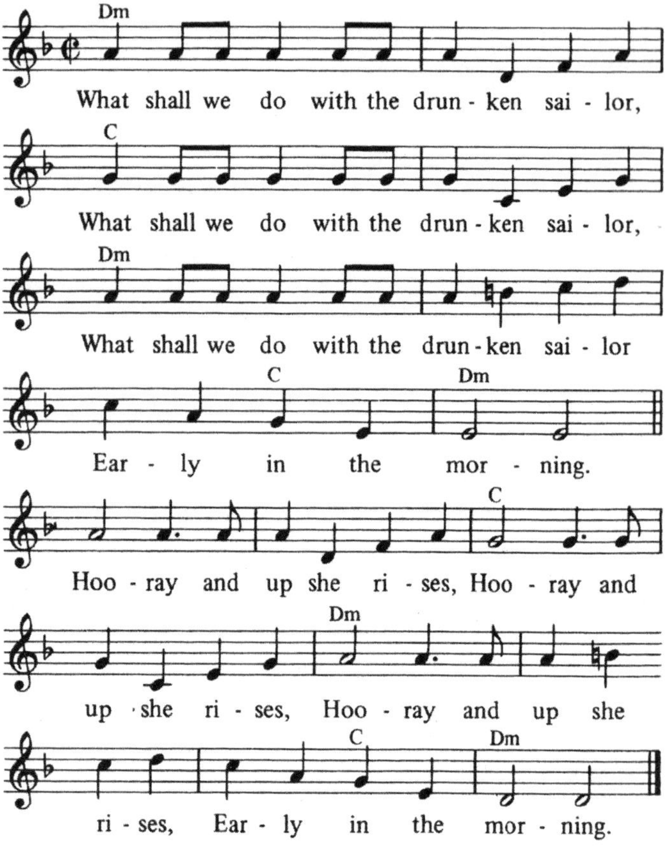
Dm
What shall we do with the drun - ken sai - lor,
C
What shall we do with the drun - ken sai - lor,
Dm
What shall we do with the drun - ken sai - lor
C
Dm
Ear - ly in the mor - ning.
C
Hoo - ray and up she ri - ses, Hoo - ray and
Dm
up she ri - ses, Hoo - ray and up she
C
Dm
ri - ses, Ear - ly in the mor - ning.

ALL THE PIRATES: What shall we do with the drunken sailor,
What shall we do with the drunken sailor,
What shall we do with the drunken sailor,
Early in the morning?

Chorus: Hooray and up she rises
Hooray and up she rises
Hooray and up she rises
Early in the morning.

2. Put him in the longboat till he's sober.
3. Pull out the plug and wet him all over.
4. That's what we do with the drunken sailor.

End of act one

6 **hooray** [hʊˈreɪ] hurra – 6 **to rise** [raɪz] *hier:* hochgehen, sich heben – 10 **longboat** Beiboot – 10 **till** bis – 10 **sober** nüchtern – 11 **plug** Stöpsel – 11 **to wet** nassmachen

Act 2

The Golden Island. Pineapple and Coconut are sitting on a bench. In the background is the jungle.

Pineapple:	I'm tired.
Coconut:	Tired of what?
Pineapple:	I'm tired of this island.
Coconut:	I'm tired of it, too.
Pineapple:	Life is boring here.
Coconut:	And we can't do anything about it. How can we get away?
Pineapple:	We haven't got a boat.
Coconut:	And we can't build a boat. Nothing but palm trees, orange trees, and monkeys ... it's terrible!
Pineapple:	Perhaps we must stay here for the rest of our lives.
Coconut:	Oh, don't say that!
Pineapple:	Just think . .. you must stay here for the rest of your life.
Coconut:	Please don't talk about it or I'll cry. *(Peach comes in from the right.)*
Peach:	What's the matter with you two?
Pineapple:	It's so boring here.
Coconut:	Yes, so boring.
Peach:	That's terrible. What can we do to make you happy again?
Coconut:	Find a boat … any boat … it must only sail.
Peach:	A boat? You know that's impossible. We haven't got one and we can't make

2 **bench** (Sitz-)Bank – 2 **jungle** ['dʒʌŋgl] Dschungel – 4 **to be tired of** ['taɪəd] *hier:* von etw. genug haben, etw. satt haben – 7 **boring** langweilig – 10 **boat** [bəʊt] Boot – 12 **palm tree** [pɑːm] Palme – 13 **monkey** ['mʌŋkɪ] Affe

one. We must stay here, and we must make the best of it.

Coconut: Please don't talk about it or I'll cry.

Peach: You must see the sunny side. You don't have to work. There's a lot of food. There are coconuts everywhere and as much fruit as we can eat.

Pineapple: I know. That's the problem. We eat … we sleep … we eat … we sleep.

Coconut: And when we wake up, we eat again. Eat and sleep, walk in the jungle and go to the beach. That's all. What a life!

Pineapple: It's boring, very boring, and I'm fed up!

Coconut: You said it.

(Banana comes in from right.)

Banana: Hello.

(They don't answer.)

Hello? What's the matter?

Peach : They need help … just look at them.

Banana: Why?

Peach: They are fed up with this island.

Banana: Oh, I see. Then I know what we can do.

PEACH:	What is it?
BANANA:	We can only do one thing.
PEACH:	What's that?
BANANA:	Have a party. Let's have a party with songs, and food and drink. They will be happy after that, I'm sure.
PEACH:	We'll have fresh coconut milk and lots of fruit.
BANANA:	*(shouts)*
	Hello … everyone … come on … we're going to have a party. Get the coconut milk.
PEACH:	And the bananas, and the peaches, and the pineapples.
	(*Peanut, Orange, and Lemon come along with some of the other people from the island. They are carrying food and drink.*
	Everyone talks to each other.)
1ST PERSON:	Have a banana.
2ND PERSON:	Oh, I'd like one.
3RD PERSON:	Who's got the peanuts?
4TH PERSON:	Here you are.
3RD PERSON:	I'm nuts about peanuts.
5TH PERSON:	This peach is lovely.
6TH PERSON:	I'd like a hamburger.
7TH PERSON:	And I'd like a milk-shake.
8TH PERSON:	We've only got some coconut milk-shake. I'm afraid.
ORANGE:	Quiet please. It's time for a song.
LEMON:	Good idea. One of the songs from the island.

24 **to be nuts about s. th.** ganz verrückt sein nach/auf etw.

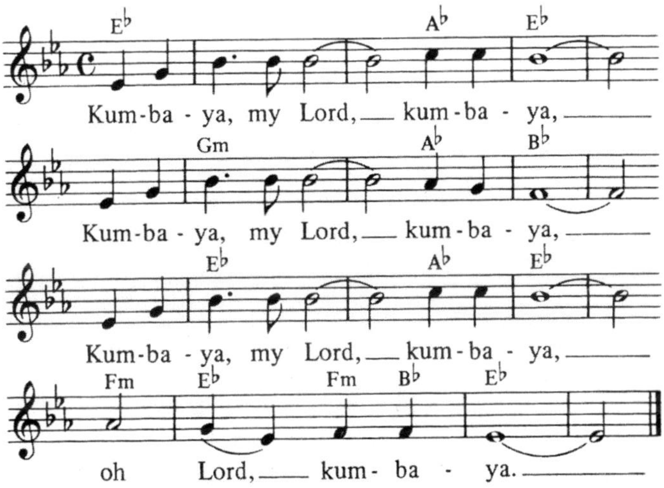

E♭	=	Es
A♭	=	As
Gm	=	g
B♭	=	B
Fm	=	f

EVERYONE: Kumbaya, my Lord, Kumbaya,
Kumbaya, my Lord, Kumbaya,
Kumbaya, my Lord, Kumbaya,
Oh, Lord, Kumbaya.
Someone's singing, Lord, Kumbaya.
Oh, Lord, Kumbaya.
Someone's praying, Lord, Kumbaya.
Oh, Lord, Kumbaya.
Someone's sleeping, Lord, Kumbaya.
Oh, Lord, Kumbaya.
Kumbaya, my Lord, Kumbaya.
Oh, Lord, Kumbaya.

1 **Kumbaya** ['kʊmbʌja] im Englisch der früheren Negersklaven: **"come down here to me"** – 1 **Lord** Gott (in der Anrede) – 7 **to pray** [preɪ] beten

Peanut: *(looks to the side and points)* Look! What's that? … over there … behind those trees!

Orange: People. Are they friends or enemies?

Lemon: They're coming this way. Be quiet. Say nothing. Shsh. *(One-Eye, Bigmouth, and Claw come in from the right, they are looking from the right to the left and back with their hands above their eyes. They don't notice the inhabitants until they are standing in front of them.)*

Claw: *(He sees the inhabitants.)* Look! Natives!

Bigmouth: But the captain said this was a desert island.

One-Eye: I think he was wrong.

Bigmouth: What are we going to do?

Claw: Take it easy. Cannonball knows. That's enough for me.

One-Eye: Shut up.

Bigmouth: Then say something.

1 **to point** zeigen – 14 **native** [ˈneɪtɪv] Eingeborene(r) – 21 **Shut up** Halt's Maul

ONE-EYE: No. I don't think they understand English.

BIGMOUTH: Then do something.

ONE-EYE: Let's shake hands. I hope they're friendly. I hope they don't bite.

(One-Eye shakes hands with Peanut.)

PEANUT: Good afternoon.

ONE-EYE: What?

PEANUT: Good afternoon. Welcome to the Golden Island.

ONE-EYE: Thank you.

(All the inhabitants get up.)

PEANUT: Please don't be afraid. We're not going to eat you. We don't eat people at all. We are the friendly people of the Golden Island.

BIGMOUTH: But we thought this was a desert island.

ORANGE: Why have you come here?

BIGMOUTH: Why we … er … yes … good question … er … why did we come?

ONE-EYE: Well, … er … we came to get some fresh water and fresh food.

ORANGE: You can get water from the river. Just follow that path through the jungle.

(points to the left)

LEMON: And we have lots of coconuts on the beach.

ORANGE: Where are your bottles?

CLAW: Bottles?

ORANGE: Yes, bottles for the water.

CLAW: Just take it easy. Cannonball knows. That's enough for me.

4 **to shake** [ʃeɪk] schütteln – 5 **to bite** [baɪt] beissen – 25 **path** [pɑːθ] Weg

One-Eye: Yes, the bottles, yes. Cannonball's got the bottles. He's on his way. He'll soon be here … I hope.

Orange: I see.

Banana: I'd like to help you.

Peanut: Yes, I'd like to help you, too.

Banana: You talked about food. Would you like some bananas?

Claw: Oh yes, thank you.

Pineapple: And what about some pineapples?

Claw: Oh yes, we love pineapples.

Peach: And would you like some sugar cane?

Claw: Oh yes, we love sugar cane.

Coconut: And coconuts?

Claw: Oh yes, we love coconuts.

Peanut: Do you like peanuts?

Claw: Oh, yes, we love peanuts.

Bigmouth: Then let's go and get some.

Peach: Is your boat on the beach?

Claw: Yes it is … it's not very far away.

Peach: Good. And is your ship near here?

Claw: Yes, it's in the next bay.

Peach: Good. Well, we'll bring all the food down to the beach. See you later.

Pineapple: See you later.
(Coconut, Peach, Banana, Peanut, and the other inhabitants leave to the right.)

Pineapple: You asked for water too, right?

Bigmouth: Yes, we did, fresh water.

Pineapple: Then I'll show you where you can find it. Come on. The river's this way. Follow me.
(Pineapple, Bigmouth, Claw and One-Eye leave to the left.)

Orange: I didn't like them.

12 **sugar cane** [keɪn] Zuckerrohr – 22 **bay** [beɪ] Bucht

LEMON: You're right. They're terrible.
ORANGE: Nobody liked them.
LEMON: That's why nobody told them who we really are.
ORANGE: I think they're pirates.
LEMON: Yes, they are.
ORANGE: And they think that we're natives.
LEMON: Let's not tell them the truth.
ORANGE: I think you're right. Let's go and find the others and warn them.
LEMON: We must think of a plan.
ORANGE: We must think of something.
(They leave to the right. Bigmouth, Claw, and One-Eye come in from the left.)
ONE-EYE: Now we know where we can find water.
BIGMOUTH: Yes. And these natives will bring the food down to the beach.
ONE-EYE: We must only do one more thing … find the treasure.
BIGMOUTH: Do you think they are real natives?
ONE-EYE: Of course they are.

10 **to warn** [wɔːn] warnen – 22 **real** echt, wirklich

Bigmouth: I'm not so sure. I think I'll ask Cannonball.

(Cannonball and Crossbone come in from the right. Crossbone is carrying a bottle in one hand and in the other a rope. It is round Kate's and Jack's necks.)

One-Eye: Hello, Captain, have you met the natives?

Cannonball: Yes, I have.

Bigmouth: Can I ask you a question, Captain?

Cannonball: Sure!

Bigmouth: It's about these natives, Captain. They all speak English. Don't you think that's strange?

Cannonball: No, of course not. Everyone speaks English.

Bigmouth: But Captain, why do they speak English? They're natives and live on a desert island.

Cannonball: And so what? What should they speak? … nativish? … Can you speak nativish? Keep your big mouth shut, Bigmouth.

Claw: Take it easy. Cannonball knows. That's enough for me.

Bigmouth: OK, you're the boss.

Cannonball: Don't worry. Be happy. We'll leave soon.

(to Crossbone)

Keep an eye on our two prisoners. I'm going to have a look at the river. Come on.

(Cannonball, Bigmouth, One-Eye and Claw leave to the left.)

7 **neck** Hals

CROSSBONE: Sit down.
(Kate and Jack sit down on the bench. Crossbone drinks.)

JACK: What are you going to do with us?

CROSSBONE: Just wait and see.

KATE: Are you going to kill us?

CROSSBONE: No. We've got a much better idea.

JACK: Will you …

CROSSBONE: Shut up.
(He drinks, yawns, and falls asleep.)

KATE: He's sleeping now.

JACK: Let's run away.

KATE: Impossible. They'll find us in no time.

BANANA: *(Banana, Orange, and Lemon come in from the right.)*
Look at them. What's that round their necks?

ORANGE: I think it's a rope.

LEMON: Why have you got a rope round your necks?

KATE: Shshsh – we're prisoners. Stowaways.

JACK: Our uncle left a will. And those pirates stole it.

LEMON: A will?

KATE: We tried to get it back.

LEMON: And what did your uncle leave in his will?

JACK: Treasure … hidden treasure. And now, tell us who are you? Are you natives?

BANANA: No, we're not natives. We are sailors. We were on the good ship Marigold. There was a storm.

LEMON: It was the worst weather of my life.

ORANGE: The waves were like mountains.

6 **to kill** töten – 10 **to yawn** [jɔːn] gähnen – 10 **to fall asleep** einschlafen – 34 **wave** [weɪv] Welle

BANANA: It was a hurricane. The ship sank.

ORANGE: But we didn't die. The waves carried us ashore … all of us … except one.

LEMON: Poor Bill.

KATE: Bill? Not Old Bill?

LEMON: Yes, Old Bill.

KATE: The pirates on The White Skeleton saved Old Bill. And Old Bill was our uncle.

LEMON: Was?

JACK: Yes … Poor Uncle Bill died a month ago.
He left all the treasure to us. He thought you were all dead.

ORANGE: And now the pirates have the will and it says where the treasure is hidden.

KATE: What can we do? This is a disaster!

What can we do? This is a disaster!

ORANGE: Well, yes and no. It's not that bad. We must find a way out of that.

CROSSBONE: *(wakes up)*
What are you talking about?

LEMON: Oh, nothing much. We're just looking for our friends.

14 **dead** [ded] tot – 17 **disaster** [dɪˈzɑːstə] Katastrophe, großes Unglück

CROSSBONE: They went down to the boat with the food.

LEMON: Thank you. We'll go down to the beach and help them.

(Banana, Lemon, and Orange leave to the right. Cannonball, Bigmouth, One-Eye and Claw come from the left.)

CANNONBALL: *(to Jack and Kate)*
Don't try any tricks on me.

CROSSBONE: Captain, don't trust these people from the island.

CANNONBALL: Why not?

CROSSBONE: I'm sure they're not natives.

CANNONBALL: Nonsense.

CROSSBONE: I'm warning you. These people aren't natives.

CANNONBALL: Of course they are. Look, here they are. I'll ask them.

(All the inhabitants come in from the right.)

CANNONBALL: *(To Peanut)*
Are you a native?

PEANUT: Of course I am.

CANNONBALL: *(to Banana)*
Are you a native?

BANANA: Yes. I've lived on this island all my life.

PEACH: I'm a native, too. Even my father was born here.

CANNONBALL: *(to Crossbone)*
Well, there you are. They are natives.

PEACH: *(to Crossbone)*
You don't think we are natives? Come on, everyone, let's dance our sun

10 **to trust** [trʌst] vertrauen – 14 **nonsense** ['nɒnsəns] Unsinn – 30 **there you are** da hast du's

dance. Then he'll see that we are real natives.
(They dance and shout.)

INHABITANTS: Oompa, oompa,
gogga, gogga, doompa
Oompa, oompa,
gogga, gogga, doompa
Oompa, oompa …

BANANA: OK, that's enough.
(They stop.)
Do you believe us now?

CANNONBALL: Yes, yes, yes. Is the food on board?

PEANUT: Yes, and the water, too.

CANNONBALL: *(He takes out the will.)*
Now, listen, could you do something for me? I need a little help. Please, look at this map. I'm trying to find a cave with hidden treasure. Do you know where it is?

BANANA: Oh yes, I know it well. It's full of treasure … gold, silver, and lots of jewels.

PEANUT: You can't carry it all alone. You'll need at least six strong men.

CANNONBALL: And there are six of us, that's OK.

ORANGE: *(points to the left.)*
Do you see that mountain?

CROSSBONE: It's a long way to walk.

ORANGE: Oh no, it's not that far. About two hours or so. Climb up this side of the mountain, then down the other side. You'll find the cave near two coconut palms.

LEMON: You can't miss it.

CANNONBALL: Thank you.

18 **cave** [keɪv] Höhle – 21 **silver** Silber – 22 **jewels** ['dʒuːəlz] Juwelen

PEANUT: When you come back, dinner will be ready. Then you can sit down and relax.

THE PIRATES: Thank you.

(The pirates leave to the left.)

INHABITANTS: Goodbye, Good luck.

(They all wave goodbye.)

KATE: Why did you tell them? It was a secret.

PEANUT: Don't worry. When they get to the cave, they'll get the surprise of their life. It's empty!

COCONUT: Look what we have got here. We've got all the treasure.

(Banana and Orange bring out a large sack.)

You can have Bill's part.

(Kate and Jack put their hands in the sack.)

PEACH: No, wait. We can't stay a moment longer. We must get down to the beach and row out to the ship, The White Skeleton.

PEANUT: But before we go, we'll get dinner ready for those pirates.

(Peanut puts some fruit on the bench.)

3 **to relax** ['rɪlæks] sich entspannen, ausspannen – 6 **good luck** viel Glück – 7 **to wave** [weɪv] winken – 10 **surprise** [sə'praɪz] Überraschung

BANANA: And when they come back, they can sit down and relax for the rest of their lives.

PINEAPPLE: They can eat and sleep and eat and sleep.

COCONUT: They can have as many bananas as they want.

PEACH: But they'll never get any treasure.

KATE: They don't know it, but they have just started the longest holiday of their lives!

JACK: And we're going home!
(They all leave to the right and sing.)

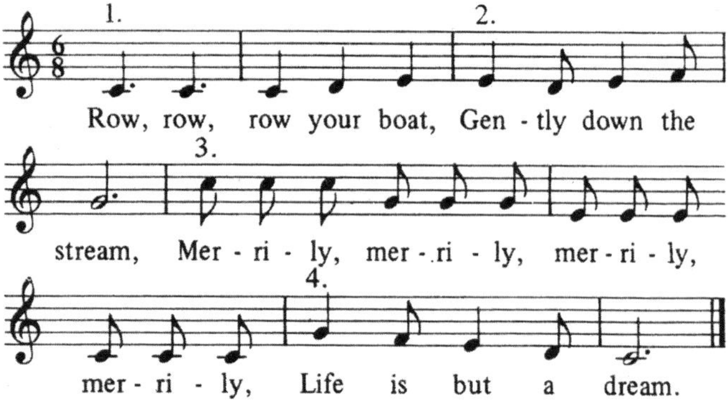

EVERYONE: Row, row, row your boat,
Gently down the stream.
Merrily, merrily, merrily, merrily
Life is but a dream.
(They sing until everyone has left the stage.)

3 **lives** [laɪvz] *Pluralform von* **life** Leben – 15 **gently** [dʒentlɪ] sanft, ruhig – 15 **stream** [striːm] Strom, großer Fluss